Ecopreneurs
Inspiring Stories of Women in Sustainability

Jacqueline Yvonne Kelly

Table of Contents

1. Introduction 2
2. Unmasking the Ecopreneurs: The Women Behind the Change 3
    2.1. The Burgeoning World of Women Ecopreneurs 3
    2.2. Trailblazers Setting the Course 4
    2.3. The Ripple Effect of Green Leadership 4
    2.4. Stories of Grit and Determination 5
3. Historical Milestones: A Timeline of Women Ecopreneurs 6
    3.1. The Early Beginnings 6
    3.2. Post-War Era: Rise of Environmentalism 6
    3.3. Late 20th Century: Expansion of Sustainable Industries 7
    3.4. The New Millennium: Climate Activists & Innovators 7
    3.5. Present Day: Looking Towards the Future 8
4. Pioneers in Green: Inspiring Stories from Leading Ecopreneurs 10
    4.1. The Trailblazing Maven: Rachel Carson 10
    4.2. The Queen of Waste Reduction: Bea Johnson 11
    4.3. The Underwater Advocate: Sylvia Earle 11
    4.4. The Eco-fashion Revolutionary: Stella McCartney 11
5. Innovative Breakthroughs: Female-led Solutions for Sustainability 13
    5.1. Bursting the Bubble: A Shift From Single-Use Plastics 13
    5.2. Powering Change: Invention of a Cost-Effective, Portable Solar Cooker 14
    5.3. Cleaner Textiles: Addressing Fast Fashion Woes 14
    5.4. Green Construction: Pioneering Sustainable Building Materials 15
    5.5. Sowing Seeds of Sustainability: Innovative Farming Technologies 15
6. The Challenges of Green Entrepreneurship: A Woman's

Perspective 17
   6.1. Obstacles in Green Entrepreneurship 17
   6.2. The Female Perspective in Green Entrepreneurship 18
   6.3. Overcoming Challenges: Resilience and Strength 19
   6.4. Conclusion: A woman's journey in green entrepreneurship . 19

7. The Power of Networking: Women's Collective Impact on Sustainability 21
   7.1. The Rise of the Green Network 21
   7.2. The Impact of Women-led Networks on Sustainability ... 22
   7.3. Case Studies: A Closer Look at Women's Green Networks ... 22
   7.4. Engaging in Green Networking: A Guide for Aspiring Women Ecopreneurs 23
   7.5. Conclusion: The Power of the Collective 23

8. Strategies for Success: Lessons from Successful Women Ecopreneurs 25
   8.1. Trailblazing Techniques: Echoing Success 25
   8.2. Building a Green Brand: Storytelling and Transparency 26
   8.3. Extensive Research: Key to Innovation 26
   8.4. Persistence and Resilience: The Unseen MVPs 27
   8.5. Embracing Partnership & Collaboration 27

9. Young Visionaries: Next-Generation Women in Sustainability ... 29
   9.1. Courageous Innovators: Challenging the Status Quo 29
   9.2. Navigating the Green Labyrinth: Success amid Challenges .. 30
   9.3. Mentoring the Future: Inspiring the Next Wave of Ecopreneurs 30
   9.4. Visibility and Recognition: Celebrating Green Achievements 31

10. The Future of Sustainability: Trends Shaped by Women Ecopreneurs 33
   10.1. Technological Innovation for Sustainability 33

 10.2. Circular Economy - Reinventing Traditional Business Practices 34
 10.3. Green Building and Urban Planning 34
 10.4. Impact Investing 34
 10.5. Resilient and Inclusive Communities 35
 10.6. Food Sustainability 35

11. From Passion to Action: Your Guide to Becoming an Ecopreneur 37
 11.1. Discovering Your Sustainability Passion 37
 11.2. Formulating a Sustainable Business Idea 38
 11.3. Testing and Validating Your Business Idea 38
 11.4. Developing a Comprehensive Business Plan 39
 11.5. Assembling Your Green Team 39
 11.6. Launching Your Green Venture 40

We are living on this planet as if we had another one to go to.

— Terry Swearingen

Chapter 1. Introduction

Immerse yourself in our Special Report on "Ecopreneurs: Inspiring Stories of Women in Sustainability"! This isn't just a report – it's a vibrant burst of inspiring stories, real-world experiences, and valuable insights gained from the journeys of women who have made significant strides in the field of sustainability. Take a deep dive into their challenges, endeavors, and triumphs. Uncover the secrets of their sustainable success and learn how these eco-warriors are reshaping our world, one eco-friendly innovation at a time. From industry pioneers to young visionaries, their narratives are as diverse as they are dynamic. Prepare to be inspired and educated on how you too can make a lasting positive impact on our planet. Make no mistake – this Special Report will not only enlighten you, but also urge you to embark on your very own ecopreneurial journey. Hurry, it's time to let these inspiring stories fuel your sustainability-driven mission!

Chapter 2. Unmasking the Ecopreneurs: The Women Behind the Change

The earliest seeds of ecopreneurship take root in the resilience and tenacity of women who dared to chart a different course. Their indefatigable spirit and relentless pursuit of sustainability contribute to the evolving landscape of green entrepreneurship. They stand as remarkable beacons of hope, lighting a path toward a more sustainable future for all.

2.1. The Burgeoning World of Women Ecopreneurs

Venturing into the world of ecopreneurship is no walk in the park – rather, it is a thrilling roller coaster ride filled with unpredictable turns, invigorating climbs, and dizzying descents. The eco-warriors featured in this report have confronted the tumultuous voyage head-on, transforming obstacles into opportunities and leading from the front in their sustainability-focused endeavours.

These women ecopreneurs represent a multitude of industries and sectors, spanning the realms of sustainable energy, recycling technology, eco-friendly fashion, sustainable food production, and much more. Regardless of their domain, they all share a common thread: a profound commitment to environmental preservation, a dedication to sustainable innovation, and a daring entrepreneurial spirit.

2.2. Trailblazers Setting the Course

The role of women ecopreneurs in reshaping how we interact with the environment cannot be overstated. They serve as vanguards on the frontline of a global green movement, with many of them pioneering groundbreaking advancements that redefine industry norms and create opportunities for sustainable growth. These women visionaries proclaim a compelling narrative: not only can businesses be profitable, but they can also promote ecological soundness.

Despite the persistent challenges women face in the business world – unequal access to funding, resources, and opportunities; sociocultural biases; and, often, the struggle to balance personal and professional commitments – these ecopreneurs have managed to ascend on their growth trajectory, shattering glass ceilings and outdated conventions along their journey.

2.3. The Ripple Effect of Green Leadership

The power of these women leaders in the sustainable sector extends far beyond their individual enterprises. Through their tireless efforts, they inspire a new generation of ecopreneurs to lead the charge towards a sustainable future. They provide a roadmap for others to follow, proving that environmental stewardship can go hand in hand with successful entrepreneurship.

The impact of these ecopreneurs also reverberates through the economy and society at large. By creating jobs that uphold sustainable principles, they foster an environment for economic growth which respects planetary boundaries. They play a pivotal role in raising public awareness about the urgency of sustainable living and actively contribute to the shaping of policies and regulations that promote green practices.

2.4. Stories of Grit and Determination

The women ecopreneurs' stories shared in this report are teeming with the grit, resilience, and determination necessary to bring about positive environmental change. These narratives paint a vivid picture of their trailblazing journey, showcasing not just their notable achievements but also recounting the myriad challenges they had to surmount. Through these tales, they illuminate the path to sustainable success, exemplifying the power of perseverance, creativity, and genuine concern for the environment.

As you delve into the last chapter of this report, you will encounter a myriad of encouraging and enlightening anecdotes, candid confessions, and insightful observations. Each woman's unique story is a testament to her passion for sustainability, her drive to initiate change, and her commitment to foster a better world.

Their enduring efforts pay testimony to the transformative power of ecopreneurship, urging more women to step forward, seize the helm, and deliver on the promise of sustainability. Their narratives evoke a call to action, inspiring each of us to play our part in safeguarding our planet and to champion a cause bigger than ourselves. It turns out, ecopreneurship is not just about transforming businesses; it's about revolutionising the way we inhabit our world.

Remember: every transformative journey begins with a single step. Thus, let their stories move you. Learn from their experiences. Embrace their wisdom. And dare to stride forward on your personal journey to become an ecopreneur. The future of our planet, after all, lies in our collective hands. A sustainable future awaits us – it's high time we took the leap and jumped into the fray.

Chapter 3. Historical Milestones: A Timeline of Women Ecopreneurs

It is with great appreciation that we look back onto the trajectory of female entrepreneurs in the field of sustainability, or rather, ecopreneurs. The history of these pioneers is rich and has significantly influenced the direction of the sustainability industry. By reflecting upon this lineage, we hope to gain invaluable insights into the evolution and development of ecopreneurship and the integral role played by women in this movement.

3.1. The Early Beginnings

It all started in the late 19th century with pioneers like Beatrix Potter and Ellen Swallow Richards. Potter wasn't just the author of the well-loved Peter Rabbit series, but also an ardent conservationist who, after acquiring a considerable amount of land in the Lake District, ended up leaving it to the National Trust, thus securing its future as a place of untouched, natural beauty.

Meanwhile, on the other side of the Atlantic, Ellen Swallow Richards, a formidable chemist and environmentalist, can be rightly credited as one of the mothers of sustainability. Her work played a vital role in recognizing and mapping out waste and pollution and pushing for cleaner alternatives and efficient waste management.

3.2. Post-War Era: Rise of Environmentalism

Fast-forwarding to the post-war era, as the environmental

implications of large-scale industrialization became more apparent, the roles and responsibilities of ecopreneurs evolved as well. Women like Rachel Carson, an American marine biologist and author, profoundly impacted environmental policy and sparked public awareness on environmental issues with her groundbreaking book "Silent Spring". She highlighted the destructive effects of pesticides, leading to a nationwide ban on DDT and other harmful pesticides.

During the same era, Elinor Ostrom, an American political economist, passionately explored how communities can manage shared resources system sustainably without external, central authorities. Her work earned her a Nobel Prize in Economic Sciences, the only woman to have achieved this feat till date.

3.3. Late 20th Century: Expansion of Sustainable Industries

The late 20th century witnessed an explosion of women leading sustainable industries. For instance, Anita Roddick, the founder of the Body Shop, played an instrumental role in demonstrating ethical and sustainable consumerism. Her vision led to the promotion of natural beauty products, reduction of packaging waste, and championing fair trade practices.

Around the same time, we saw the advent of green building pioneers such as Amory Lovins, a British environmental scientist who championed the passive solar movement and co-founded the Rocky Mountain Institute, a think tank focused on sustainable development.

3.4. The New Millennium: Climate Activists & Innovators

The turn of the century marked a dramatic shift towards the urgency and mobilization of efforts against climate change. Women ecopreneurs like Majora Carter started leading the way by initiating urban revitalization projects with sustainable living at its heart, addressing issues of environmental justice in low-income communities.

Innovators also emerged, with leaders like Elon Musk's ex-wife, Justine Musk, who used her influence to invest in and promote cleaner technologies and sustainable ways of living. Meanwhile, Sarah Kauss, the founder of S'well, revolutionized the reusable water bottle industry, tackling plastic pollution head-on.

3.5. Present Day: Looking Towards the Future

Today, we find ourselves in an era where the narrative is not only about women taking part but leading ecological entrepreneurship. Women ecopreneurs are now more than ever at the forefront of innovating sustainable solutions, advocating for policy changes, and driving businesses that are both economically profitable and environmentally friendly.

Showcasing individuals such as Christiana Figueres who led the global negotiations for the critical Paris Agreement of 2015, highlighting the work of women-led sustainability startups such as Uncharted Power, founded by Jessica O. Matthews, which focuses on clean, renewable energy solutions, or tribute to Emily Penn, an ocean advocate and skipper who is leading the fight against plastic pollution in our seas, proves that the future of sustainability is, indeed, female.

As we travel this incredible timeline of women ecopreneurs, we learn that their stories are not just about the date they started or the milestones they've achieved; it's about the sweat, the resilience, and the unwavering hope that they carry for the planet's future. These women, their challenges overcome, and their victories, represent the journey of sustainability—a journey that is far from over and continues to inspire and drive present and future generations of ecopreneurs.

Our historical understanding and appreciation of women ecopreneurs' past contributions provide the impetus and inspiration for future sustainable endeavors. This drives home the point that sustainable change is not only possible but is already being enacted by these formidable women.

Chapter 4. Pioneers in Green: Inspiring Stories from Leading Ecopreneurs

Commencing directly on the topic of 'Pioneers in Green: Inspiring Stories from Leading Ecopreneurs', we are presented with a treasure trove of narratives that beautifully showcases the resilience, innovation, and dogged determination of exceptional women leading the charge in environmental sustainability. These vanguards in eco-conscious entrepreneurship, or 'ecopreneurs', have not only challenged the status quo but have been instrumental in paving the way to a more sustainable future.

4.1. The Trailblazing Maven: Rachel Carson

Let's start with the remarkable story of Rachel Carson. Known as the mother of the modern environmental movement, Carson was instrumental in igniting a widespread public interest in environmental issues back in the 1960s. Her groundbreaking book, 'Silent Spring', highlighted the dire consequences of pesticide use, leading directly to a nationwide ban on DDT and other harmful pesticides. Carson's courageous crusade against powerful chemical companies and her unwavering belief in the right of the public to know about environmental damage have immortalized her as a true pioneer in environmental sustainability. Her endeavors proved instrumental in creating a paradigm shift in how society perceives environmental conservation, spawning a new generation of environmentally conscious leaders and ecopreneurs.

4.2. The Queen of Waste Reduction: Bea Johnson

Next in line is Bea Johnson, a visionary who has single-handedly revolutionized our understanding of waste and consumer responsibility. Known as the 'queen of the zero waste lifestyle', Johnson, with her bold initiatives, has given a whole new meaning to sustainable living. Her book, 'Zero Waste Home', allows an intimate glimpse into her life, where she and her family produce not more than a quart of waste in an entire year. By prioritizing experiences over possessions, Johnson has inspired many around the globe to reduce their environmental footprint, laying down a blueprint for minimal waste existence.

4.3. The Underwater Advocate: Sylvia Earle

On course of exploring the varied terrain of ecopreneurship, we simply cannot ignore Sylvia Earle, the legendary oceanographer. An awe-inspiring combination of scientific genius and prolific environmental advocacy, Earle has spent the better part of her life underwater. She not only holds the record for the deepest untethered ocean dive but has been relentlessly using her platforms to raise awareness about the vital importance of our world's oceans. Her non-profit organization, Mission Blue, supports marine protected areas, or 'Hope Spots', essential for the health of the ocean, which she rightfully refers to as the "blue heart of the planet."

4.4. The Eco-fashion Revolutionary: Stella McCartney

More recently, the world of fashion has been graced by the presence of a game-changing ecopreneur, Stella McCartney. Not only did she revolutionize the luxury fashion landscape with her eponymous brand, but she brought sustainability to the forefront of the industry. Known for her steadfast refusal to use fur or leather in her designs, much before it became 'cool', McCartney stands as a paragon of eco-conscious fashion entrepreneurship. Her commitment to ethical sourcing, innovative use of materials, and minimization of waste has sparked a sea change in an industry notorious for its environmental footprint.

From Rachel Carson's prophetic warnings against environmental damage, Bea Johnson's radical reimagination of consumer behavior, Sylvia Earle's tireless devotion to ocean conservation to Stella McCartney's emphatic creation of eco-conscious luxury fashion, we are fortunate to witness pioneering women who are not just passionate about environmental sustainability but are actively transforming this passion into tangible, impactful actions.

Each of these women ecopreneurs did not merely adopt a 'green' lifestyle, but truly embedded sustainability into the core of their professional and personal journeys. This chapter shows that all these pioneering efforts are interconnected, reminding us that sustainability is not just a movement, but a necessary lifestyle choice that reflects our respect and care for the planet we inhabit.

As you move on to the following chapters, remember these powerful narratives; draw on them for inspiration and as a testament to what is achievable. May their stories be your launchpad as you embark on your unique ecopreneurial journey. That trail has been blazed, showing us that if we dare to dream of a healthier earth, we too can be the catalysts to make it a reality. For, after all, as Rachel Carson said, "In nature, nothing exists alone." And in this shared existence, we must all play our part.

Chapter 5. Innovative Breakthroughs: Female-led Solutions for Sustainability

As our collective awakening to the importance of sustainable living continues to grow, a plethora of innovative solutions are coming to the forefront. Remarkably, many of these breakthroughs are propelled by determined women who are leveraging their skills, vision, and tenacity to reshape the world we live in. This chapter dives deep into the realm of female-led sustainability innovations, exploring the practicalities, the technology, the impact, and the stories behind these pioneering breakthroughs.

5.1. Bursting the Bubble: A Shift From Single-Use Plastics

One ubiquitous challenge facing our environment is the overreliance on single-use plastics. However, an innovative solution has emerged from the mind of innovative ecopreneur Hollie Webb. Seeing the need to transition from disposable, non-biodegradable plastic containers, she founded her company, EcoCup, a firm specializing in the production of biodegradable food and drink containers made from plant-based materials.

At EcoCup, raw polylactic acid (PLA), derived from renewable resources such as sugarcane and corn starch, is used instead of petroleum-based plastics. The company's products, even though they resemble traditional plastics in functionality and resilience, completely decompose under composting conditions within 180 days, signaling a promising trend towards a more sustainable future.

5.2. Powering Change: Invention of a Cost-Effective, Portable Solar Cooker

Solar power is widely acknowledged for its potential to provide sustainable energy solutions. Resolute to harness this potential for the vulnerable, Catlin Powers, co-founder and CEO of One Earth Designs, developed SolSource, a highly efficient and portable solar-powered cooker.

Simply put, SolSource uses highly reflective surfaces to concentrate sunlight, thus generating heat enough to cook food or boil water. The product, which is portable, durable, and free from running costs, has been a game-changer in off-grid communities. Not only does it provide a much-needed, affordable, and sustainable solution for clean cooking, but it also reduces the need for biomass fuels, thus helping combat deforestation and related health issues.

5.3. Cleaner Textiles: Addressing Fast Fashion Woes

Fast fashion is another notorious contributor to pollution and waste. To counteract this, Iris Smeekes founded ReCircle, a revolutionary textile recycling company that employs advanced technology to recycle used clothes.

ReCircle's innovative process includes a proprietary technique that can efficiently separate and recover the materials in blended fabric garments. The recovered materials are then spun into new, high-quality yarns, which can be used again in the production of new clothes. Consequently, this innovative circular system stands to mitigate the environmental impact of the fashion industry significantly, reducing waste and dependency on virgin resources.

5.4. Green Construction: Pioneering Sustainable Building Materials

In the field of construction, Sandra Kwak's 10Power is making inroads by promoting the use of renewable energy in developing countries. The company aims to replace traditional, toxic, and non-renewable building materials with a wide range of more sustainable alternatives. This includes the use of recycled plastics for construction blocks and mushroom-based alternatives for packaging and insulation.

kwak's approach to green construction aims to address the monumental task of reducing the carbon footprint in the highly emission-intensive construction sector. By providing a scalable, cost-efficient, and environmentally sound alternative, 10Power seeks to lead the transition towards a more sustainable future in construction.

5.5. Sowing Seeds of Sustainability: Innovative Farming Technologies

Farming and food production also provide opportunities for environmentally friendly innovation. Sarah Bellos, founder of Stony Creek Colors, offers a sustainable solution by producing natural indigo dye for denim manufacturers. This initiative replaces synthetic dyes made from petroleum with plant-based dyes made from Indigofera suffruticosa, a crop Bellos grows herself.

Bellos' method not only supplies an eco-friendly dye but also promotes better farming practices, as growing indigo helps improve soil quality and reduce water pollution. By doing so, Bellos deciphers the enormous potential enclosed in sustainable farming technologies, driving a much-needed shift in the coloring component of the textile industry.

In conclusion, these examples serve as a testament to the potential of innovative sustainability solutions led by women. From revolutionizing materials and methods used in everyday items like containers and textiles to addressing critical issues in energy use, construction, and food production — female ecopreneurs are at the forefront of pioneering a more harmonious existence with our planet. Their inspiring stories of success show the triumph of determination, vision, and ingenuity over the daunting challenges our world faces today. As we move forward, these innovative breakthroughs light our path towards a truly sustainable future.

Chapter 6. The Challenges of Green Entrepreneurship: A Woman's Perspective

Green entrepreneurship, also known as ecopreneurship, challenges the traditional view of a linear economy - where materials are mined, used, and then thrown away - by promoting a circular, sustainable economy where waste is minimized and resources are continually reused. This chapter focuses intensively on the challenges faced by women engaging in green entrepreneurship. It provides an in-depth and comprehensive exploration of the hurdles they have to overcome, their strengths and their resilience in face of adversity, and the unique perspective they bring to the field.

6.1. Obstacles in Green Entrepreneurship

While every entrepreneur faces challenges, those in the field of sustainability often face unique obstacles that can make their journey particularly tough. These problems can range from a lack of financial support and market receptivity to structural issues or legal roadblocks. The complexities of transforming innovative green ideas into practical, marketable products or services can be daunting. This section provides an extensive look into these challenges and also sheds light on how women ecopreneurs navigate these complex roads.

Traditional investors may hesitate to support green businesses due to perceived risks or a lack of knowledge about the industry. Many ecopreneurs need to spend considerable time and effort educating potential investors about their product, service, or business model. Moreover, sustainable materials and technologies can be expensive, contributing to higher costs that need strategic planning and even more innovative thinking to mitigate.

Green entrepreneurs also often contend with regulatory challenges. Legislation may not be fully supportive or understanding of green business models, which may hinder progress. For example, laws might favor established industries and make it hard for innovative, disruptive green businesses to compete.

Another key challenge is consumer attitudes and market acceptance. Despite rising awareness about sustainability, many consumers still prioritize price and convenience. This necessitates a significant amount of consumer education on the part of the green entrepreneurs.

6.2. The Female Perspective in Green Entrepreneurship

Women face additional hurdles in entrepreneurship due to entrenched social and cultural norms. Many women entrepreneurs struggle to be taken seriously or to navigate expectations tied to gender roles. Access to finance can also be more difficult for women due to these traditional norms. There can also be a lack of female role models in certain sectors.

For women in green entrepreneurship, these challenges can be intensified by those unique to the eco-business realm. However, women also bring strength, resilience, and a unique perspective to the field.

Women often approach business with a deep sense of social responsibility and an inclination towards sustainability, which aligns well with the values inherent in green entrepreneurship. Women are historically caregivers and tend to be more risk-averse, which can result in businesses that are more attuned to their impact on the community and the environment.

6.3. Overcoming Challenges: Resilience and Strength

Despite the many challenges faced, women in green entrepreneurship also represent stories of resilience, strength, and innovation. This section provides detailed examples of women who have overcome the aforementioned obstacles through creativity, persistence, and a spirit of defiance. Many have displayed immense resourcefulness, leveraging networks and partnerships to secure funding and mentorship opportunities.

Women ecopreneurs have also demonstrated notable tenacity, effectively breaking down complex sustainability concepts into relatable messages to change consumer attitudes.

They have pioneered solutions, created ecosystems, and showed immense courage, proving that despite the many challenges, success in green entrepreneurship is not only possible but also offers a pathway to transform our world.

6.4. Conclusion: A woman's journey in green entrepreneurship

In conclusion, while women in sustainability face both the general challenges of entrepreneurship and specific obstacles in the green sector, they bring a unique perspective and strength to the field. Their experiences offer valuable insights that can inspire and guide others.

Determined, creative, and resilient, they unleash innovative solutions that go beyond pure profit, woven deeply with purpose and a strong commitment to the betterment of our planet. Their narratives evoke admiration and inspiration, propelling more individuals - men and women alike – to join the green movement and make a difference in their own way.

Indeed, with every challenge they overcome, women ecopreneurs demonstrate the very essence of entrepreneurship - the audacity to disrupt, innovate, and effect substantial positive change. As much as their journey is fraught with difficulties, it is also marked by significant achievements and heroic tales of triumph against the odds.

After all, the essence of a heroic tale lies not in an absence of adversity, but in the audacious spirit that rises above it. Women in green entrepreneurship continue to author such tales, inspiring countless others in their wake. Their challenges are substantial, but their spirit, tenacity, and accomplishments are monumental, testifying to the profound impact they are making in reshaping our world towards sustainability.

Chapter 7. The Power of Networking: Women's Collective Impact on Sustainability

This chapter delves into the significance of networking and illuminates how the collective power and collaboration of women across the globe create a formidable impact on sustainability. It is a testament to the strength of communities, the spirit of collaboration, and the shared vision of a greener world.

7.1. The Rise of the Green Network

At first glance, networking may appear to be a simple tradition of exchanging business cards and polite pleasantries. In truth, it is much more profound. The business context has elevated networking from mere social interactions to strategic bridges for exchanging ideas, building relationships, and fostering collaboration. The green movement is no exception. Women eco-entrepreneurs worldwide have been harnessing this power to create a vibrant and dynamic network — an interconnected web of green initiatives.

The fundamentally social nature of human beings has been a cornerstone of networking. With shared ideologies and common goals, women ecopreneurs have found not just colleagues in their network - but allies. These relationships and collaborations have been fundamental in creating waves of change, influencing policy, and driving sustainability on a larger scale.

As the world started recognizing the climate crisis, women ecopreneurs also began banding together. They realized that to make tangible changes, they needed a collective, unified front. They needed to pool their innovations, strategies, and experiences to fight against the looming environmental challenges more effectively.

7.2. The Impact of Women-led Networks on Sustainability

Women's networks focused on sustainability are not just about fostering mutual help. They are instrumental in shaping public policy, influencing business strategies, and changing societal perceptions about environmental issues. Several environmental campaigns worldwide have noticed the power and potential of networking women in sustainability.

Particularly noteworthy is the way these networks encourage the collaborative rather than competitive spirit. Eco-businesses led by women often work hand in hand, complementing each other's strategies and uniting for the greater good. This cooperative essence of networking significantly deviates from the traditional, more adversarial business landscape.

7.3. Case Studies: A Closer Look at Women's Green Networks

Several organizations, cooperatives, and networks led by women are making significant strides in the realm of sustainability. For example, the Women's Environment and Development Organization (WEDO) pushes for women's rights in environmental and development policy worldwide. WEDO harnesses the power of the network and empowers women around the globe. Another prolific example is the Women in Green Forum, which brings together women from various sectors who are devoted to sustainability. Their annual gatherings create valuable channels for knowledge exchange, brainstorming, and collaboration.

Such networks showcase the collective strength of women ecopreneurs. Their alliances are not only facilitating mutual growth but are also influencing policies, driving innovations, and propelling the global sustainability movement forward.

7.4. Engaging in Green Networking: A Guide for Aspiring Women Ecopreneurs

Networking in sustainability needs a strategic approach. Understand your goals, be clear about your vision, and know what you can offer others. Attend relevant events, actively seek out potential allies, and nurture relationships. Remember, effective networking is about giving as much as receiving.

Online platforms can be wonderful tools for networking. In this digital age, physical boundaries are irrelevant. Social media platforms, virtual conferences, and online forums can connect you with potential mentors, collaborators, and like-minded individuals from around the world.

Finally, always be prepared to learn and evolve. Every connection you make can teach you something new and valuable. Networking is not just about climbing the ladder — it's a journey of perpetual learning, expanding horizons, and continuous evolution.

7.5. Conclusion: The Power of the Collective

The green movement has taught us that unity and solidarity are our most valuable weapons against environmental challenges. Networking magnifies the impact of individual actions and creates a ripple effect of change. When women ecopreneurs join hands and share a collective passion for sustainability, it results in a powerful force that propels the world towards an eco-friendly future.

This chapter emphasizes the potency and immense potential of networking in the recovery and restoration of our environment. It sheds light on the collective efforts of women worldwide united towards the common goal of sustainability. It reinforces the belief that together, we can make substantial strides in protecting the earth and ensuring a livable future.

Chapter 8. Strategies for Success: Lessons from Successful Women Ecopreneurs

A myriad of successful women ecopreneurs grace our planet today—individuals who have overcome obstacles, achieved monumental success, and set impressive precedents in the realm of sustainable entrepreneurship. Each of these prolific environmental pioneers harbor distinctive strategies for success, cultivated from years of experience and continuous learning.

8.1. Trailblazing Techniques: Echoing Success

Every journey towards success begins somewhere. Consider the story of Yvon Chouinard, founder of outdoor clothing company Patagonia. She began with a simple but potent belief in reconnecting people with nature. Her primary strategy was to instill this ethos into her company's DNA, committing to donate a portion of their profits to environmental causes. This form of 'cause marketing' stimulated both their reputation and sales, evidencing that fiscal success and environmental stewardship can go hand in hand.

To mirror such successes, emerging ecopreneurs must identify the core values and beliefs that shape their eco-conscious drive. This foundational principle serves as a compass, guiding decisions and promoting a resonant brand image, thereby engaging their audience with a cause beyond the product or service.

8.2. Building a Green Brand: Storytelling and Transparency

Successful ecopreneurs often harness the power of storytelling and transparency to build a green brand. Rachel Carson, renowned marine biologist and conservationist, utilized this in her groundbreaking book, "Silent Spring." By effectively communicating the ecological implications of pesticide use, she influenced the global conversation about environmental issues and fueled legislative changes.

In the modern business milieu, transparency becomes an invaluable asset. Showcasing the sustainable aspects of production processes, origin of materials, and how profits are reinvested into environmental causes can all build a green brand's credibility. Many consumers today prioritize environmental friendliness and social responsibility, making transparency a must-have trait for any ecopreneur.

8.3. Extensive Research: Key to Innovation

A key lesson that can be learned from the successes of female ecopreneurs is the value of extensive, strategic research. Ellen MacArthur harnessed the power of research to establish the Ellen MacArthur Foundation which works towards accelerating the transition to a circular economy. Addressing such a complex issue demanded a deep level of understanding and the application of sustainable practices on a systemic level. Her extensive research and holistic approach were undeniably crucial factors to her success.

Investing resources, time, and effort into understanding market needs, the nature and impact of the problem you're addressing, and the most innovative, sustainable solutions can be game-changing.

8.4. Persistence and Resilience: The Unseen MVPs

The journeys of successful eco-entrepreneurs are largely marked by unwavering persistence and resilience. Take for instance, Majora Carter, who transformed her environmental justice advocacy into a thriving business model by launching the Majora Carter Group, a consulting firm dedicated to poverty alleviation and sustainable development.

Her persistence and resilience were tested when she set upon the uphill battle of changing the public perception and institutional bias against low-status communities. But she persisted, and her continued resilience led to a cascade of successes, including the creation of the Sustainable South Bronx and Hunts Point Riverside Park.

For emerging ecopreneurs, your resilience can define your journey. Be prepared for inevitable setbacks and in the face of adversity, continue forward. Use that resistance as a catalyst to evolve, innovate, and strengthen your mission.

8.5. Embracing Partnership & Collaboration

Large-scale environmental challenges often require collaborative interventions. Dr. Wangari Maathai, founder of the Green Belt Movement (GBM) in Kenya, well understood the power of collaboration. Her initiative enlisted the help of Kenyan women to plant trees, combating deforestation and improving quality of life.

In the world of business, alliances and partnerships can amplify the positive impact and scale of sustainable initiatives. Whether it's collaborating with other businesses for sustainability campaigns or partnering with non-governmental organizations (NGOs) for broader environmental goals, alliances can be a potent force for change.

In summation, the path to ecopreneurial success is densely populated with valuable insights. By aligning their brand with their purpose, maximizing transparency, conducting extensive research, embodying resilience, and embracing collaboration, aspiring women in sustainability can chart out their trajectory for success, echoing the victories of these successful women ecopreneurs.

Chapter 9. Young Visionaries: Next-Generation Women in Sustainability

In an era where sustainability challenges escalate with each passing day, a wave of youthful enthusiasm and innovation sweeps across the globe, renewing our hope in a sustainable future. The young visionaries, the next-generation women in sustainability, stand at the helm of this wave, diligently crafting eco-friendly solutions, reaching past conventions, and beaconing an era of responsible, creative entrepreneurship.

9.1. Courageous Innovators: Challenging the Status Quo

Leading the ranks of change-makers are young women who dare to think differently. Their accomplishments underscore their daring mindset, challenging the inherited worldviews and unproductive systems. One such notable ecopreneur is Miranda Wang, the Co-founder and CEO of BioCellection, a groundbreaking venture that converts unrecyclable plastic waste into sustainable chemicals. Bothered by the massive amount of plastic waste generated by her hometown community in Vancouver, Wang set forth her path of innovation, propelling her to become a driving force in sustainable entrepreneurship.

Another courageous innovator is Emily Cunningham, the Co-founder of Wildtype, engaged in the development of cell-cultivated seafood products. Wildtype's mission revolves around reducing overfishing and providing a sustainable alternative that eliminates the need for fishing in the wild. These leaders embody sheer courage and an innovative mindset, indeed setting an example for future generations.

9.2. Navigating the Green Labyrinth: Success amid Challenges

Venturing into the realm of ecopreneurship is often fraught with hurdles and complexities. However, many young women ecopreneurs have continued to navigate the green labyrinth and have achieved remarkable success. Hannah Herbst, the creator of BEACON (Bringing Electricity Access to Countries through Ocean Energy), at just 15 years old identified a source of renewable energy from ocean currents. Her device aims to provide electricity to developing countries, marking a significant development towards achieving sustainability.

Another inspiring figure is Ugandan entrepreneur Vanessa Nakate, founder of the Youth for Future Africa and the Rise Up Movement. Despite the numerous existential hurdles, her commitment to turning the tide on climate crisis has led her to international forums including the Davos 2020 conference. The journeys of these women make it clear that patience, resilience, and belief in one's mission are integral to success in this field.

9.3. Mentoring the Future: Inspiring the Next Wave of Ecopreneurs

The role of mentorship in inspiring the next wave of ecopreneurs is essential. Young leaders like Kehkashan Basu, a global influencer and founder of Green Hope Foundation, has leveraged her platform to engage and educate younger generations on environmental challenges. Through workshops, conferences, and stewardship initiatives, Basu has mentored a wave of young environmental activists, proving the profound impact mentorship can beget.

Another influential figure is Gitanjali Rao, Time's first-ever 'Kid of the Year.' An inventor, scientist, and advocate, Rao has actively engaged in promoting clean water, cybersecurity, and opioid addiction management through cutting-edge technology. She is a powerful example for budding ecopreneurs that age is not a barrier in making a significant impact.

9.4. Visibility and Recognition: Celebrating Green Achievements

The saga of the next-generation women in sustainability is incomplete without acknowledging the global recognition these mission-driven ecopreneurs have procured. Organisations and initiatives like the United Nations Environment Programme's 'Young Champions of the Earth,' Ashoka Youth Venture, and the Global Student Entrepreneur Awards are bestowing young visionaries with newfound visibility and global platforms.

These global acknowledgments underscore the significant triumphs of these ecopreneurs, speak volumes about their invaluable contribution, and highlight the impact of their sustainable innovations on global communities.

To summarise, the narrative of young visionaries in sustainability is inspiring, impressive, and continually evolving. Through their courage and innovation, these next-generation women are breaking new ground, dissolving barriers, overcoming challenges, and most importantly, working relentlessly to secure a sustainable future for all. Their stories, rich with lessons and insights, serve as beacons of hope and motivation for anyone ready to embark on a journey toward ecopreneurship. This chapter could mark the beginning of your journey of making a difference in the world you inhabit. Let their experiences guide your steps, their triumphs fuel your dreams, and their wisdom shape your path. It is, indeed, the time to look forward to a greener, healthier world sculpted by these young visionaries in sustainability.

Chapter 10. The Future of Sustainability: Trends Shaped by Women Ecopreneurs

We start off by entering the realm of the ecopreneur's vision, their predictions for the future of sustainability, and the groundbreaking paradigms that have emerged under their determined leadership, nourished by their undying commitment to a greener future. Broadly, we focus on the trends being forged by these formidable industry-leaders, carving out a dynamic yet sustainable landscape for generations to come.

10.1. Technological Innovation for Sustainability

The intersection of technology and sustainability has unveiled a plethora of opportunities, and women ecopreneurs have been quick to embrace and harness these. From blockchain systems that promote supply chain transparency, to Artificial Intelligence(AI)-driven analytics optimizing resource consumption, futuristic tech has become an intrinsic part of their sustainability blueprints. Innovations like solar-powered smart windows, biodegradable packaging, and clean energy solutions, encapsulate the zealous pursuit of these women to merge digital advancement with environmental considerations, for fostering an eco-friendly metamorphosis of the modern lifestyle.

10.2. Circular Economy - Reinventing Traditional Business Practices

At the heart of ecopreneurship lies the essence of circular economy. Rejecting the traditional, linear 'take-make-waste' economic model, ecopreneurs have championed the implementation of circular, regenerative strategies in businesses. Key features being emphasized include reducing material inputs, recycling waste, lowering energy consumption, and increasing service life. Top women ecopreneurs have shown us that reshaping our consumption habits and rethinking waste can lead to unprecedented profitability, while ensuring environmental resilience.

10.3. Green Building and Urban Planning

The push toward urban sustainability has intensified, with ecopreneurs leading the call to sustainable architecture and better urban planning. Their efforts aim at reducing the carbon footprint of urban sprawls, promoting energy and water efficiency in buildings, and overall improving inhabitants' lifestyle while preserving the environment. They envisage cities filled with green buildings, vertical farming skyscrapers, and eco-friendly public transportation.

10.4. Impact Investing

Driven by the dual objective of yielding financial return while generating positive societal impact, impact investing has gained momentum. Prominent women ecopreneurs are leveraging their financial acumen to direct capital towards sustainable business endeavors that address the world's pressing environmental issues.

This not only boosts sustainable development but also advances female empowerment in the financial world.

10.5. Resilient and Inclusive Communities

A wealth of women ecopreneurs have committed to build resilient communities that thrive on shared prosperity, equality, and ecological integrity. By pushing for policies and practices that ensure equitable resources distribution and foster social inclusivity, these women are spearheading the creation of resilient communities that can withstand environmental and societal pressures.

10.6. Food Sustainability

The agriculture and food industry has not escaped the keen eyes of ecopreneurs either. Regenerative agriculture, plant-based diets, reducing food waste, and responsibly sourced food are just some ways these women are working to stabilize our planet's food system. Driven by their respect for the earth and its bounty, they are tirelessly advocating sustainable food practices.

In conclusion, women ecopreneurs aren't just paving new paths for sustainable practices, they're building entire highways, directing us towards a more sustainable and prosperous future. Their stories inspire and remind us that change is possible, and it starts with us. Their work speaks volumes about their determination, innovation, and their endless battle for a cause they ardently believe in. As we march ahead, hand-in-hand with these outstanding women at the helm of sustainability, we can look forward to a future that promises not only technological growth, but also well-being for our planet and its inhabitants. In the grand narrative of sustainability, their endeavors weave an invigorating tale of motivation, reinforcing the fact that every small effort counts in preserving our world. Their inspiring journey as successful ecopreneurs urges us all to contribute towards this global mission of sustainability, enabling us to usher in the much-needed change.

Chapter 11. From Passion to Action: Your Guide to Becoming an Ecopreneur

The transition from passion to action, from authenticity vested in personal values to the implicated endeavor of entrepreneurship, is a substantial journey of self-identification, exploration, and significant hard work. As an aspirant ecopreneur, the pursuit of sustainability blended with entrepreneurship combines your fervent drive for protecting the environment with the exciting world of creating and managing your own business. This chapter invites you to initiate that journey, offering comprehensive guidance on merging your passion for sustainability with the journey to becoming an accomplished ecopreneur.

11.1. Discovering Your Sustainability Passion

Unearthing your passion for sustainability is usually the first step towards becoming an ecopreneur. Recognizing your fervor towards preserving the environment, reducing waste, or promoting eco-conscious choices leads to a realization of your passions which can ultimately be transformed into action. Soul-searching prompts and personal anecdotes aplenty will arrive at your doorstep, guiding you to identify your calling.

Your passion may be rooted in numerous facets of sustainability, including but not limited to reduction of carbon footprint, fostering biodiversity, advocating for renewable energy, or promoting sustainable products or services. Don't worry about being niche-specific; instead, strive for aligning with the broader spectrum of sustainability, allowing for evolution and refinement of your passion as you progress in your ecopreneurial journey.

11.2. Formulating a Sustainable Business Idea

After identifying your passion for sustainability, the next step is to transform that passion into a sustainable business idea. It's about marrying your passion with a tangible need in the market. Your business idea may involve creating sustainable products, providing eco-friendly services, facilitating environmental education, or promoting green technology, among others.

Keep in mind that sustainable business model innovation involves mastering the art of balancing ecological, social, and economic aspects. This requires an understanding of the customer's needs, the value propositions you're aiming to offer, and the employment of various activities, resources, and partnerships to deliver those. It also involves creating an economic and sustainable return for your business.

11.3. Testing and Validating Your Business Idea

Once you have a business idea ready, it's time to test and validate it. This stage involves carrying out detailed market research, performing a SWOT (Strengths, Weaknesses, Opportunities, Threats) analysis, and assessing the financial feasibility of your business. Action-oriented steps such as offering your product/service to a small group for initial feedback, pitching your idea to potential investors, or even doing an informal survey within your network can provide initial validation. Validating your ideas early can potentially save you from significant future headaches, making this a critical step in your journey.

It's also essential to assess the sustainability impact of your business idea. A tool like Life Cycle Assessment (LCA) can help you evaluate the environmental implications of a product or service throughout its lifespan.

11.4. Developing a Comprehensive Business Plan

After validation, it is time to formulate a comprehensive business plan. A cogently articulated business plan outlines the objectives, strategies, and critical timelines of your venture. It should encompass components like market analysis, competitor's assessment, your unique selling proposition (USP), marketing and sales strategy, operational plans, and financial forecasts.

Importantly, the business plan should vividly reflect your commitment towards sustainability. Clearly explain the environmental and social benefits your venture plans to bring, how you aim to make your operations green, and your strategies to promote responsible consumer consumption.

11.5. Assembling Your Green Team

Behind every successful ecopreneur, there is a team of dedicated individuals adhering to the cause, contributing their unique skills and perspectives. When assembling your team, you should look for people who not only possess the required skills but also share your passion for sustainability.

Establish a culture that aligns with your company's sustainable visions. Innovation, transparency, respect for nature, and ethical practices should be the core tenets of your organizational culture. A green team that operates with a shared purpose will stand as the foundation of your sustainable venture.

11.6. Launching Your Green Venture

Finally, the moment of setting your green venture into motion is upon you. Extensive planning, continuous effort, and rigorous preparations culminate here. However, remember that launching your venture is just the beginning of your ecopreneurial journey.

As you commence operations, expect to meet challenges that would require you to adapt and modify your strategies. Having a flexible mindset and a resilient attitude are characteristics of successful ecopreneurs. Harness your passion continuously and let it guide you in creating a prosperous venture that benefits society and aids in the preservation of our ecosystem.

The journey from passion to action, threading through the cabinet of self-discovery, sustainable innovation, resolute decision-making, and continuous learning, is a gratifying yet intensive passage. Embrace its nuances and challenges as part of the game; remember, every successful ecopreneur started once where you are standing now. Be patient, enjoy the process, stay committed to your cause, and celebrate every milestone, for every tiny victory leads you closer to becoming an inspiring force in the world of sustainability.

www.ingramcontent.com/pod-product-compliance
Lightning Source LLC
Chambersburg PA
CBHW070951220526
45471CB00007B/2978